**W9-BYI-076**

Dear Parents and Educators,

Welcome to Penguin Young Readers! As parents and educators, you know that each child develops at his or her own pace—in terms of speech, critical thinking, and, of course, reading. Penguin Young Readers recognizes this fact. As a result, each Penguin Young Readers book is assigned a traditional easy-to-read level (1–4) as well as a Guided Reading Level (A–P). Both of these systems will help you choose the right book for your child. Please refer to the back of each book for specific leveling information. Penguin Young Readers features esteemed authors and illustrators, stories about favorite characters, fascinating nonfiction, and more!

## The Star-Spangled Banner

LEVEL **4**

GUIDED READING LEVEL **N**

This book is perfect for a **Fluent Reader** who:
• can read the text quickly with minimal effort;
• has good comprehension skills;
• can self-correct (can recognize when something doesn't sound right); and
• can read aloud smoothly and with expression.

Here are some **activities** you can do during and after reading this book:
• Comprehension: After reading the book, answer the following questions:
    • What do the stripes on the modern American flag represent?
    • How big is the Star-Spangled Banner? Why is it so big?
    • Why are some of the pieces of the Star-Spangled Banner missing?
    • Over the years, people have worked hard to protect the Star-Spangled Banner. What are some of the ways the flag is protected today?
• Create a Timeline: This is a nonfiction book about the Star-Spangled Banner, America's most famous flag. When you read nonfiction, you often find many dates in the text. Using the dates and facts in the book, create a timeline to show the history of the Star-Spangled Banner.

Remember, sharing the love of reading with a child is the best gift you can give!

—Bonnie Bader, EdM
    Penguin Young Readers program

*Penguin Young Readers are leveled by independent reviewers applying the standards developed by Irene Fountas and Gay Su Pinnell in *Matching Books to Readers: Using Leveled Books in Guided Reading*, Heinemann, 1999.

For all my teachers,
especially my mom and dad—NRL

PENGUIN YOUNG READERS
An Imprint of Penguin Random House LLC

Smithsonian
This trademark is owned by the Smithsonian Institution and is registered
in the U.S. Patent and Trademark Office.

Smithsonian Enterprises:
Christopher Liedel, President
Carol LeBlanc, Senior Vice President, Education and Consumer Products
Brigid Ferraro, Vice President, Education and Consumer Products
Ellen Nanney, Licensing Manager
Kealy Gordon, Product Development Manager

Photo credits: Library of Congress: 4, 7, 11, 13, 17, 27, 31, 32, 33; Maryland Historical Society: 18;
Pickersgill Retirement Community: 19; Smithsonian National Museum of American History: cover,
3, 8–9, 14, 16, 20, 21, 23, 24–25, 29, 30, 31, 32, 33, 34, 35, 36, 38, 39, 40–41, 42, 43, 44, 45, 46–47;
Smithsonian National Portrait Gallery: 12; Thinkstock: 15 © Purestock; Thinkstock/iStock:
all backgrounds and borders © vasosh.

*Library of Congress Cataloging-in-Publication Data is available.*

ISBN 978-1-101-99607-2 (pbk)          10 9 8 7 6 5 4 3 2
ISBN 978-1-101-99608-9 (hc)          10 9 8 7 6 5 4 3 2 1

# Smithsonian
# THE STAR-SPANGLED BANNER

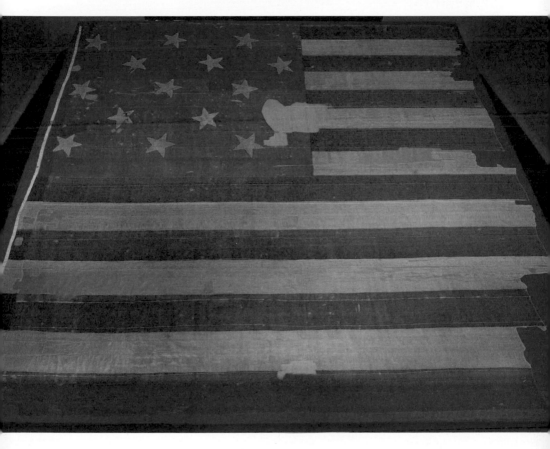

by Nancy R. Lambert

Penguin Young Readers
An Imprint of Penguin Random House

THE STAR SPANGLED BANNER.

Of  long may it wave,
Over the land of the free,
And the home of the brave,

# Contents

# The Star-Spangled Banner

Old Glory.

The Stars and Stripes.

The Red, White, and Blue.

The Star-Spangled Banner.

The American flag has many nicknames. But the Star-Spangled Banner is more than just a name.

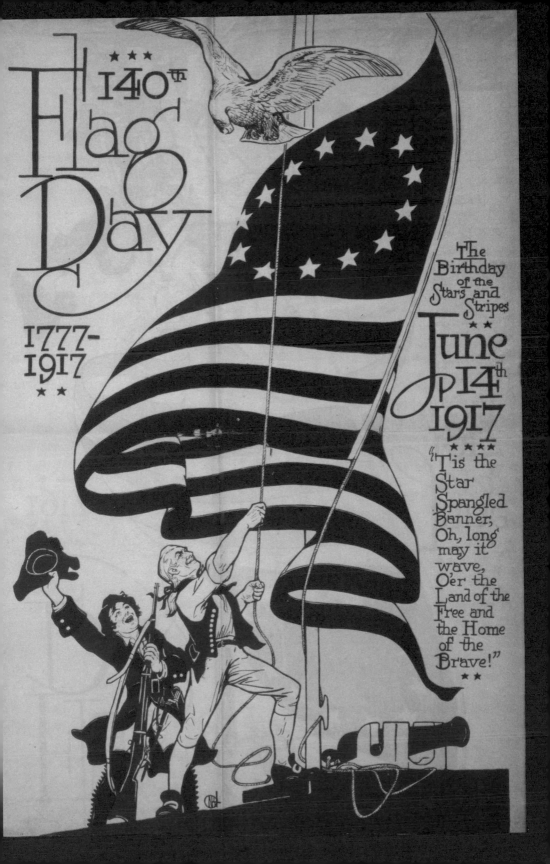

It's a real flag!

The Star-Spangled Banner is
America's most famous flag. It flew
above a fort after an important battle.
This **inspired** a lawyer to write a song.
That song became the **national anthem**
of the United States.

Fort McHenry, Baltimore, Maryland, where the Star-Spangled Banner first flew

Like all American flags, the Star-Spangled Banner is red, white, and blue. It has stars and stripes. These colors and shapes all have different meanings.

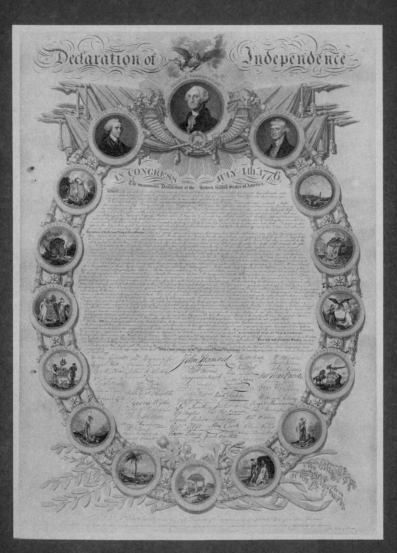

A copy of the Declaration of Independence

THE DECLARATION OF INDEPENDENCE.
JULY 4TH 1776.

Signing the Declaration of Independence in 1776

The stripes **represent** the **colonies** that fought to become their own country. They were the first states in the United States of America. The stars stand for other places that became states over time.

The Star-Spangled Banner

The Star-Spangled Banner has 15 stars and 15 stripes. But why 15 stripes? Was that a mistake?

No.

In 1794, Congress decided the flag should have 15 stripes. That later changed in 1817. Today's flag has 13 stripes and 50 stars.

The United States flag today

# War!

In 1812, the United States was at war with the British. The British captured Washington, DC, in 1814. They set fire to the Capitol Building. They even burned the White House! Next they were headed to Baltimore, Maryland.

A burned piece of wood from the White House

The British attack Washington, DC

Baltimore was an important city for American shipping. It was guarded by Fort McHenry. Lieutenant Colonel George Armistead was in charge of the fort. He was ready for the British—with soldiers, large guns, and a new flag.

# Sewing a New Flag

Lieutenant Colonel George Armistead

In 1813, Armistead had ordered two flags made for Fort McHenry. One would be used in bad weather. The other should be really, really big. Armistead wanted to be sure the British saw this American flag waving—before they even got near the fort!

Mary Pickersgill of Baltimore had sewed many kinds of flags before. Armistead hired her. Mary started sewing, along with some of her family. An African American servant worked on the flags, too. The larger flag would become the Star-Spangled Banner.

Mary Pickersgill

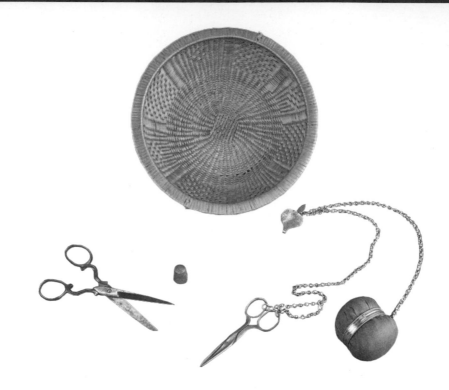

Sewing tools like the ones used to make the Star-Spangled Banner

The women sewed strips of wool together to form stripes. They cut stars from cotton. Each star was almost two feet across!

The flag was going to be 30 feet high and 42 feet long. That's as tall as a three-story building. It's longer than a school bus. And it was too big for Mary Pickersgill's house!

Mary Pickersgill's home in Baltimore, Maryland

Mary and the other women gathered all the pieces of the flag. They moved to a building across the street to work. Sometimes the women sewed until midnight.

It took several weeks to make the Star-Spangled Banner. Mary Pickersgill was paid $405.90 for the job. Many people in Baltimore did not earn that in a year!

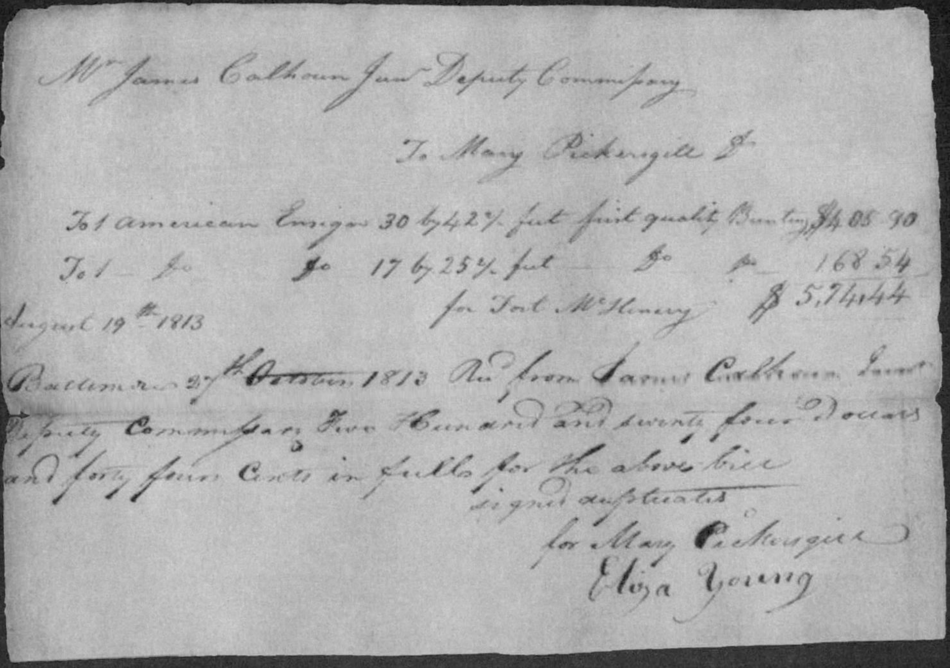

Mr James Calhoun Junr Deputy Commissary

To Mary Pickersgill Dr

To 1 American Ensign 30 by 42 feet first quality Bunting $405 90
To 1 do do 17 by 25 feet do do 168 54
for Fort McHenry $574 44
August 19th 1813

Baltimore 27th ~~October~~ 1813 Recd from James Calhoun Junr Deputy Commissary Five Hundred and seventy four Dollars and forty four Cents in full for the above bill
signed duplicates
for Mary Pickersgill
Eliza Young

A receipt for the work and materials

# Raise the Flag!

When the flag was finished, it was sent to Fort McHenry. There it was raised up high on a 90-foot pole. You could see it for miles.

A flag flies over Fort McHenry during the battle.

On September 13, 1814, the British attacked.

They sailed warships into the Baltimore harbor. For twenty-five hours, they fired bombs and rockets at Fort McHenry. Armistead and his men fought hard to defend the fort.

A British rocket

Francis Scott Key, an American lawyer, saw the whole battle. He was aboard another ship a few miles away. Key watched all night long. Through the fire and smoke, it was hard to tell who was winning. In the morning, he saw an amazing sight: an American flag was still flying!

Francis Scott Key watches the battle of Fort McHenry

Francis Scott Key was proud that the Americans had won. Since he was also a writer, he started a song right away. In it, he called the flag at Fort McHenry a "star-spangled banner." Key's poem and Mrs. Pickersgill's flag were soon to become very famous!

O say can you see, ~~through~~ by the dawn's early light,
What so proudly we hail'd at the twilight's last gleaming,
Whose broad stripes & bright stars through the perilous fight
O'er the ramparts we watch'd, were so gallantly streaming?
And the rocket's red glare, the bomb bursting in air,
Gave proof through the night that our flag was still there,
O say does that star-spangled banner yet wave
O'er the land of the free & the home of the brave?

On the shore dimly seen through the mists of the deep,
Where the foe's haughty host in dread silence reposes,
What is that which the breeze, o'er the towering steep,
As it fitfully blows, half conceals, half discloses?
Now it catches the gleam of the morning's first beam,
In full glory reflected now shines in the stream,
'Tis the star-spangled banner — O long may it wave
O'er the land of the free & the home of the brave!

And where is that band who so vauntingly swore,
That the havoc of war & the battle's confusion
A home & a Country should leave us no more?
~~Their blood has~~
Their blood has wash'd out their foul footstep's pollution.
No refuge could save the hireling & slave
From the terror of flight or the gloom of the grave,
And the star-spangled banner in triumph doth wave
O'er the land of the free & the home of the brave.

O thus be it ever when freemen shall stand
Between their lov'd home & the war's desolation!
Blest with vict'ry & peace may the heav'n rescued land
Praise the power that hath made & preserv'd us a nation!
Then conquer we must, when our cause it is just,
And this be our motto — "In God is our trust,"
And the star-spangled banner in triumph shall wave
O'er the land of the free & the home of the brave. —

Francis Scott Key wrote his song on September 14, 1814.

# From Song to Anthem

Francis Scott Key named his song "Defense of Fort M'Henry." Newspapers around the country printed it. His poem was matched with a popular tune. It was given a new title and sold as sheet music. Meanwhile, the United States won its war against the British. Now many Americans were singing "The Star-Spangled Banner."

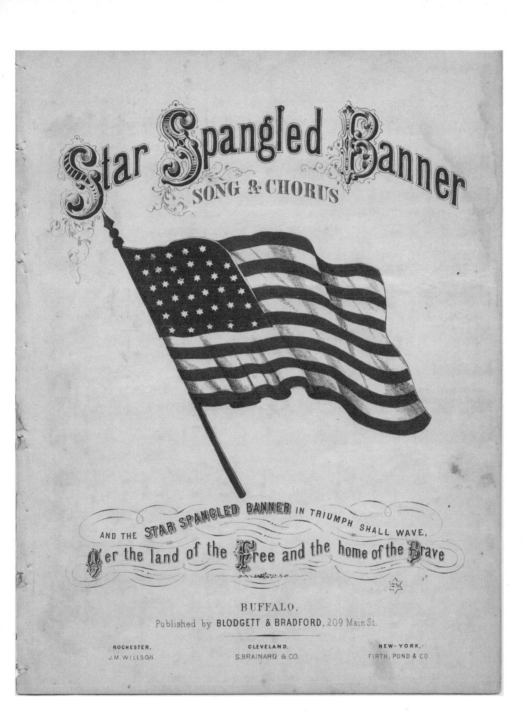

Sheet music for "The Star-Spangled Banner"

"The Star-Spangled Banner" quickly became a favorite **patriotic** song. Americans were proud of their country.

"The Star-Spangled Banner" expressed their feelings. It was often sung at public events or parades. The United States army and navy played the "The Star-Spangled Banner" when they raised and

lowered the flag each day. People stood up when the song was played at baseball games. In 1931, Congress made it the national anthem of the United States.

But what happened to the flag itself?

# A Family Flag

Lieutenant Colonel Armistead kept the flag from the battle of Fort McHenry. The Star-Spangled Banner moved to his home in Baltimore. A few years later, Armistead died. The flag was passed on to his daughter. It would stay within the family for almost 100 years.

Georgiana was the name of Armistead's daughter.

Pieces of the Star-Spangled Banner

The Armisteads kept the Star-Spangled Banner in a large cloth bag. They let it be used at parades or patriotic events. Over the years, some people asked for **souvenirs**. They were given small pieces clipped from the famous flag. Somebody even got one of the big stars!

Mrs. Armistead may have sewed this mark on the flag. It almost looks like an A.

This is the first known photo of the Star-Spangled Banner.

The Star-Spangled Banner began to wear out. The seams split. It had holes and patches. Insects had nibbled at it. Almost 200 square feet had been snipped off.

This picture was taken in Boston in 1873. One thing was now very clear: The Star-Spangled Banner was in bad shape!

Armistead's grandson, Eben Appleton, now had the flag. He saw how damaged it was. He no longer let the Star-Spangled Banner travel.

Eben stored the flag in a bank **vault** in New York. But he knew that a national treasure should not be locked away.

Eben Appleton

The Smithsonian Institution "Castle" Building, Washington, DC

He decided to give it to the Smithsonian
Institution. So the Star-Spangled Banner
moved to Washington, DC.

Hanging outside the Smithsonian, 1907

# A National Treasure

Appleton wanted the Star-Spangled Banner to stay at the Smithsonian forever. He also wanted people to still be able to see it. But the flag needed a lot of **repair** work first!

Some of the snipped pieces were found. They were given to the Smithsonian.

Others, like the cut-out star, are still missing.

The Smithsonian first **conserved** the Star-Spangled Banner in 1914. Amelia Fowler and her team sewed on a new backing. This helped hold up the flag. It took 1.7 million stitches to do the job!

Amelia Fowler (left) created a special web of stitches for the backing.

First, the Star-Spangled Banner was
**displayed** in a case at the Smithsonian.
Then it hung in a large hall on a frame
50 feet high.

The flag was cared for and cleaned. But there were still problems. Light faded the colors. Dust and changes in temperature damaged the cloth. Hanging stretched the flag.

In 1999, the Smithsonian conserved the Star-Spangled Banner again. The flag was carefully vacuumed. It was then moved to a special lab. Some conservators worked from a bridge over the flag. They used tweezers and small clippers. They removed the old backing. Other workers used a camera and microscope. They checked the flag closely for damage. Dry sponges were used to gently lift off dirt.

Vacuuming the Star-Spangled Banner

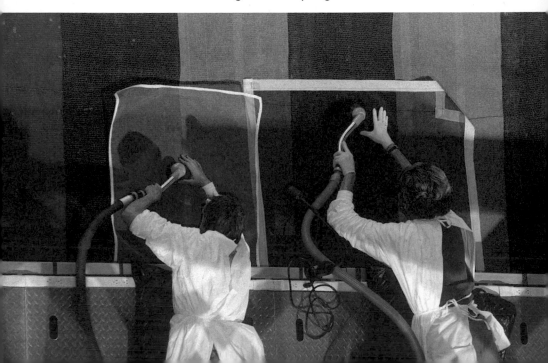

1.7 million stitches had to be snipped *off* this time.

Lying on a "bridge" to dry-sponge the flag

The workers covered every inch of the flag, slowly and carefully. The job took several years!

In 2008, the Star-Spangled Banner moved into its new home. It is displayed at the Smithsonian's National Museum of American History. The flag rests on a tilted table so visitors can see it, but it won't stretch or tear. It's in a special space where the air, temperature, and light are controlled.

Millions of people proudly hail the Star-Spangled Banner every year.

# Glossary

**anthem:** a patriotic song

**colonies:** places that are ruled by another country

**conserved:** removed dirt and added materials to clean something

**displayed:** shown

**inspired:** having a strong feeling because of something

**national:** belonging to a nation or country

**patriotic:** loving one's country

**repair:** to fix

**represent:** to stand for something

**souvenirs:** objects from a special event or place

**vault:** a locked box or room, usually in a bank